HOW A HOUSE IS BUILT

NEW AND UPDATED

BY GAIL GIBBONS

HOLIDAY HOUSE · NEW YORK

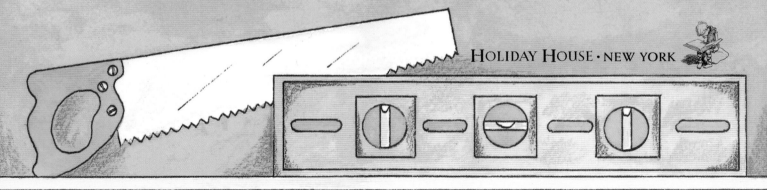

For Kent

Special thanks to Christine A. Hobson, PE, Lead Engineer, Moore Associates.

Copyright © 1990, 2020 by Gail Gibbons
All Rights Reserved
HOLIDAY HOUSE is registered in the U.S. Patent and Trademark Office.
Printed and bound in January 2020 at Tien Wah Press, Johor Bahru, Johor, Malaysia.
www.holidayhouse.com
Second Edition
1 3 5 7 9 10 8 6 4 2

Library of Congress has cataloged the prior edition as follows:

Library of Congress Cataloging-in-Publication Data

Gibbons, Gail.
How a house is built / written and illustrated by Gail Gibbons.—1st ed.
p. cm.
Summary: Describes how the surveyor, heavy machinery operators,
carpenter crew, plumbers, and other workers build a house.
ISBN 0-8234-0841-8
1. House construction—Juvenile literature.
[1. House construction.] I. Title.
TH4811.5.G53 1990
69'.837—dc20 90-55107 CIP AC
ISBN 0-8234-0841-8
ISBN 0-8234-1232-6 (pbk.)

Second Edition
ISBN: 978-0-8234-4694-0 (hardcover)
ISBN: 978-0-8234-1232-7 (paperback)

Many people live in houses.

log cabin

stone house

There are many kinds of houses.

adobe house

cinder-block house

They are built with different materials.

brick house

frame house

glass house

Houses are built in many shapes and sizes, too.

architect

This is how a wood-frame house is built. First, an architect draws plans.

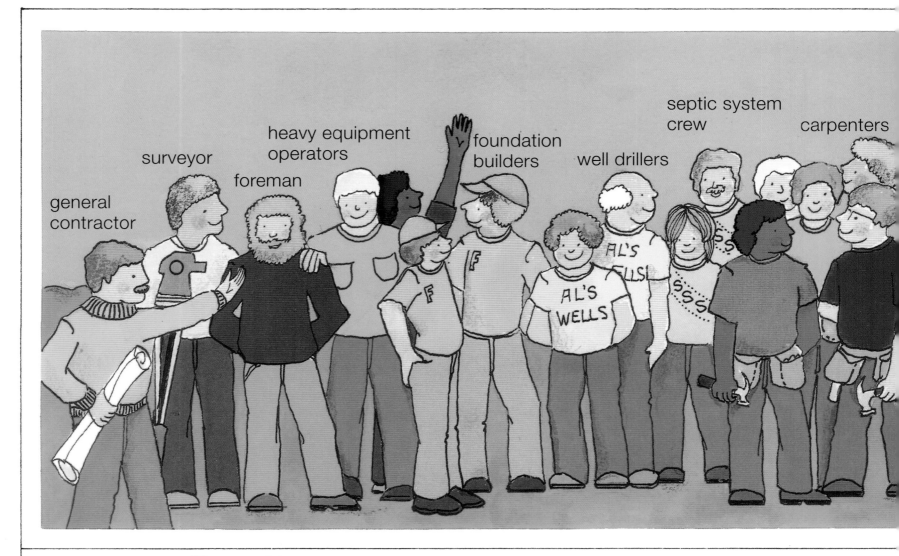

general contractor

surveyor

foreman

heavy equipment operators

foundation builders

septic system crew

carpenters

well drillers

AL'S WELLS

AL'S WELLS

The architect consults with an engineer who will be in charge of designing the frame and foundation of the house. The architect then recommends a general contractor, who will be in charge of building the house.

plumbers

mason

electricians

heating specialists

drywall crew

painters

landscapers

During the months ahead, the general contractor will hire all these people to complete the project. The general contractor makes sure everything is done according to schedule.

At the construction site, the surveyor measures for the foundation while another worker helps. Wooden stakes mark the corners of the house. A well is being drilled.

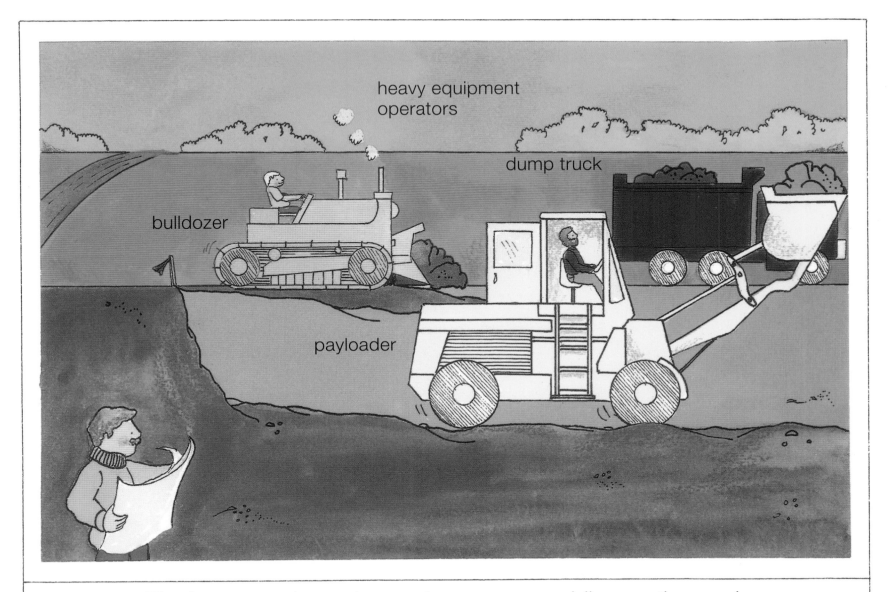

The heavy equipment operators come rumbling up the road.
They dig a hole where the foundation will go. The foundation
will support the weight of the house.

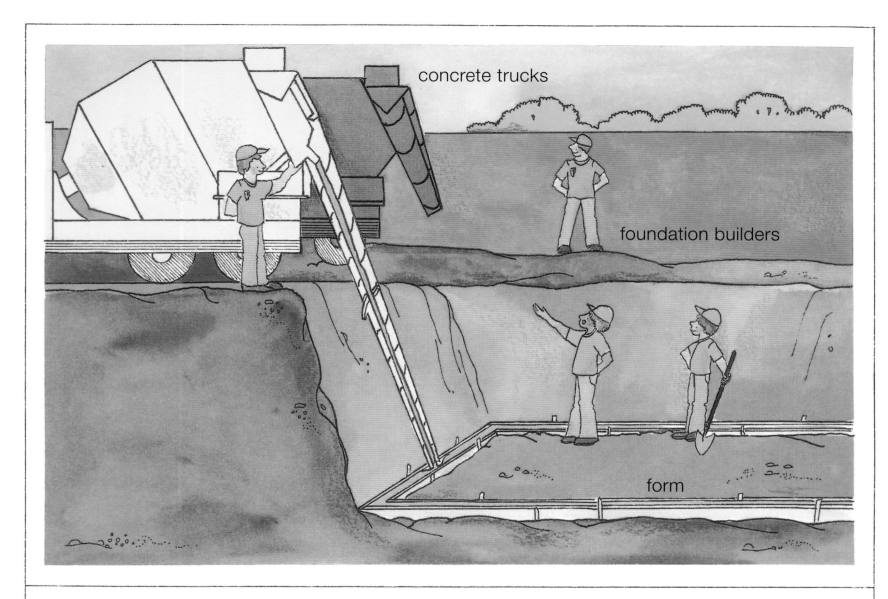

concrete trucks

foundation builders

form

Next, the foundation builders arrive. They dig trenches around the edges. Then they line the trenches with boards to make a form. Trucks move into place and pour concrete.

footing

When the concrete is hard, the boards are removed. This is the footing for the foundation. The footing will give the house a firm base.

gravel

drain

bull float

Then the foundation builders build forms on the footing for the foundation walls. The concrete trucks come and go to fill the forms. The concrete floor of the basement is poured and smoothed over.

The forms are removed when the concrete is hard. A membrane, or liner, is rolled on the outside walls so moisture can't get inside. Then the bulldozer pushes, or backfills, the dirt up against the outside of the foundation.

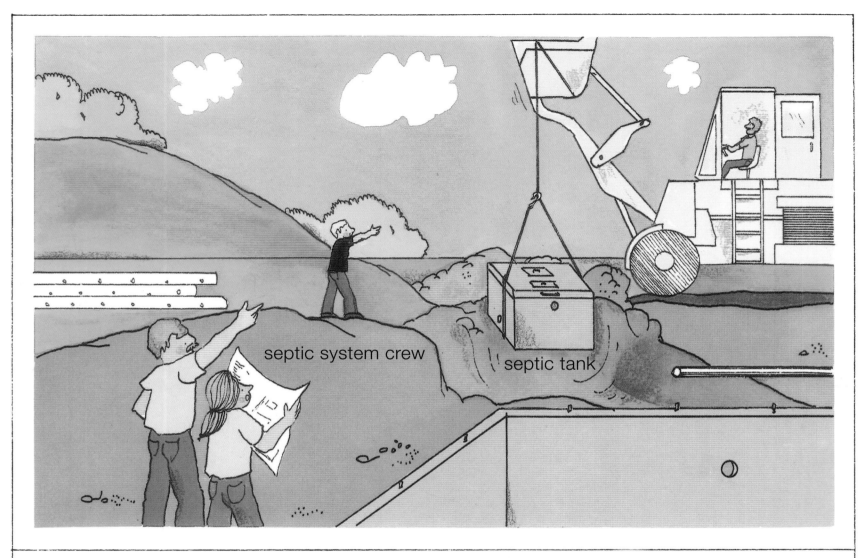

The septic system crew arrives. They dig a hole and lower a septic tank into it. A pipe goes from the basement to the septic tank. The waste from drains in the house will flow into the septic tank.

Here comes the carpenter crew. Out come their tools! They tighten down boards for the sill plate to the top of the anchor bolts on the foundation. Then they hammer heavier boards, called joists, into place.

subfloor or deck

The carpenters nail or screw down sheets of plywood to the joists, making what is called a subfloor or deck. It is the floor of the house.

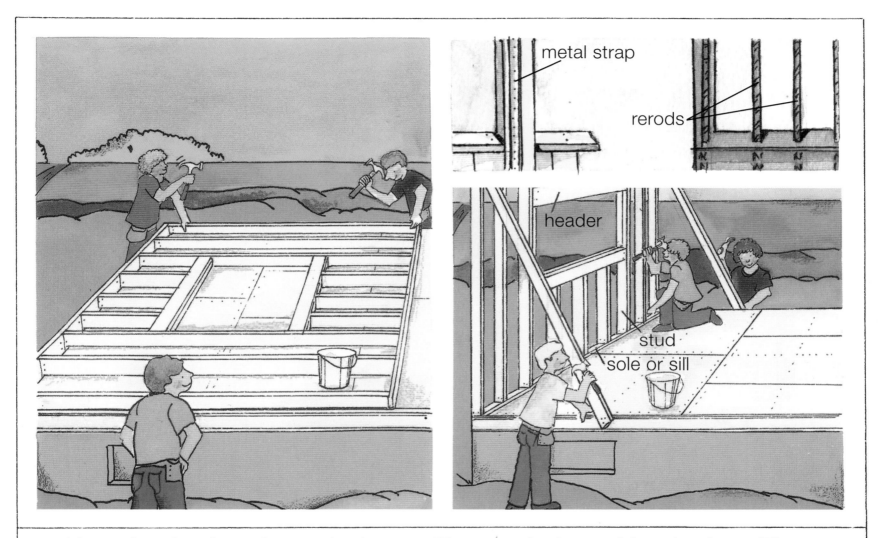

Next, they begin to frame the house. They study the architect's plans. They saw pieces of wood to their correct sizes. They nail together an outside wall of the house. The carpenter crew pushes the wall up and nails it into place. Then they nail straps along the outside that connect with the rim boards and foundation wall to protect against hurricanes and earthquakes.

Another wall goes up . . . and another!

window opening   door opening

Finally, all the walls are in place.

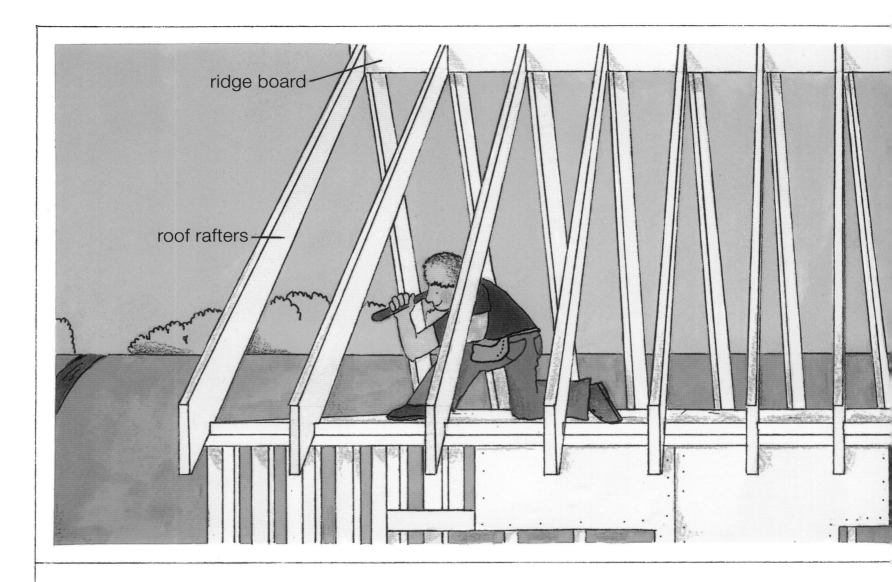

ridge board

roof rafters

Now the carpenters frame in the roof. Roof rafters are nailed to the ridge board. Soon the framing of the house will be complete.

sheathing

housewrap

They begin to enclose the house by nailing sheets of plywood to the outside of the frame. This is called sheathing. Then they saw out the spaces for the windows and doors. Housewrap is nailed to the outside of the plywood to keep moisture out.

On the roof a carpenter is busy nailing down shingles. Other carpenters nail clapboard siding to the sides of the house. Day after day the work continues.

The mason is almost finished building the chimney. Windows
and doors are installed.

Inside the house, interior walls are nailed into place. An electrician runs wire through the walls to outlets and switches. Plumbers install the pipes that bring water to faucets and carry waste from drains to the septic system.

drywall crew

switch

insulation

joint compound

Insulation is tucked between studs to keep heat inside the house. The drywall crew cuts and nails the drywall into place. They smear joint compound onto the drywall joints to make smooth walls.

Next, the finished floors are nailed down. Windows and doors
are trimmed. The painters paint the walls.

heating
specialists

Everything is almost done! The electrician hooks up the
light fixtures. Cabinets are installed. The plumber puts in
the bathtub, toilets, and sinks. The furnace and hot-air ducts
are installed.

landscapers

KEEP OFF THE GRASS

Outside, the landscapers notice that the grass they planted is beginning to grow. They dig a hole for one more bush.

For many months this has been a very busy place. At last the work is done. Now the house is ready to become a home.

SOME BUILDING FACTS

Shipping containers or canisters can also now be used to build homes.

Concrete is made up of three basic components: water; cement; and either rock, sand, or gravel.

In 1970, Congress created the Occupational Safety and Health Administration (OSHA) to assure safe and healthful working conditions for working men and women.

The sod house or "soddy" was often an alternative to the log cabin during the frontier settlement of the Great Plains of Canada and the United States. Construction of a sod house involved cutting patches of sod in rectangles and using them for walls and roofs.

Louise Blanchard Bethune (July 21, 1856–December 18, 1915) was the first American woman known to have worked as a professional architect.

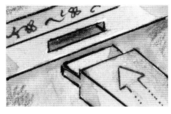
Traditional Japanese carpentry, which is more than 1,000 years old, does not rely on the use of nails. Instead, pieces of wood are fitted together. This is called "joinery."

Some homes are built from "reclaimed wood," which means that old barns and other structures are taken apart piece by piece and the lumber is used to build entire homes, or parts of them.